The Cross of Ministry

Lectures on Service and Discipleship

SAINT **SHENOUDA**PRESS

The Cross of Ministry

Lectures on Service and Discipleship

By:

Fr Bishoy Kamel

ST SHENOUDA PRESS
SYDNEY, AUSTRALIA
2024

The Cross of Ministry
Lectures of Service and Discipleship

By: Fr Bishoy Kamel

ST SHENOUDA PRESS
8419 Putty Rd,
Putty, NSW, 2330
Sydney, Australia

www.stshenoudapress.com

ISBN 13: 978-0-6457704-8-3

Cover Design:
David Georgy

Contents

Foundations of Pastoral Ministry in the Church

"'Service must begin at the cross; otherwise, it will culminate in failure. The cross embodies boundless love.'"

~ Fr Bishoy Kamel

The most important principle in pastoral ministry is love. It is the first marker of Christ's Church and the vein that connects its members. Love today requires martyrdom without the shedding of blood, while their power is no less than the blood of the martyrs. The aim of the commandment is to love from a pure heart with utmost passion.

Love must be free from hypocrisy. Do not be two-faced and speak one word within a small community and another word in the wider community.

The church is a constant source of love for all: love for the flock, sinners, poor, and even those who offend us. For example, Peter, seal of the martyrs, loved his flock, and so died in their place after he asked the soldier to kill him in prison and not in front of his children. Bishop Abraam of Fayyūm shows the example of one who loves the poor, prayed on their behalf and showed them love.

There is the love for sinners, shown in Christ's love for the prodigal son. Love for the abusers is found in the example of Stephen's prayer for those who stoned him. Signs of love are also seen in the church. All these manifestations of love rely on self-denial and crucifying the ego.

Ego and selfishness are the first enemy of love. Therefore, the sign of love is the presence of spiritual unity in the church, as the prayer of the morning watch teaches us, "I therefore, a prisoner for the Lord, urge you to walk in a manner worthy of the calling to which you have been called, with all humility and gentleness, with patience, bearing with one another in love, eager to maintain the unity of the Spirit in the bond of peace. There is one body and one Spirit—just as you were called to the one hope that belongs to your call—one Lord, one faith, one baptism" (Ephesians 4:1-5).

Both the shepherd and the servant are martyrs of love. They strive toward it in all strength derived from the crucified Christ—who loves, and continues to love, and never hates, for Love (i.e. God) never fails.

During the era of Pope Theophilus, Rome faced division, and two candidates were nominated, one of whom would be chosen for the papacy. He wrote a letter urging them to preserve the Church's unity, stressing that those striving for unity will obtain the crown of ecclesiastical unity, a crown greater than the crown of martyrdom. While the crown of martyrdom benefits the recipient, the crown of ecclesiastical unity benefits the entire Church. The adversary of good, Satan, seeks to diminish love in the Church by exposing egos, causing division. That is why the priest and servant needs to be a martyr of love between his priestly brethren and servants and the flock, living a life ridding his ego, and remaining vigilant to the adversary of good because we cannot comprehend Satan's thoughts.

We should show love for the servants, the Sunday School servants, and the church committee. All should serve together in unity. Love flourishes by engagement with spiritual work, springing from love for the cross and the One crucified, through service in the ministry, praying for everyone, and being very careful not to condemn others or glorify oneself.

Love requires effort, which the servant diligently pursues. Even Christ, out of His love, offered Himself on the cross. Love is patient, hopes for all things, and does not seek things for herself. Love is the good ground in which every Christian virtue is planted. Without love, virtue lacks validity, prayers go unheard, and ministries lose their purpose. The absence of love makes everything in the ministry a matter for the adversary of good, who sows selfishness, self-love, strife, and love of public visibility while the cross of Christ disappears.

Love is the bond that ties the shepherd to his flock, just as Christ was tied to the world through love: "God so loved the world that He gave His Son" (John 3:16). The unity of the Spirit is the nature of the one body of Christ, and we cannot partake of one body unless we are one body and members of one body. The early church used to pray as one and believed in one church, saying, "Our Father of us all, who art in heaven."

The priest and servant are a martyr of love and self-denial. This oneness of spirit embodies their learning and faith in all their services. This is the first spring from which the flock drinks, and the source of love for us should be Christ on the cross. The purpose that moves the priest and servant to serve is their love for the crucified Christ and their bond to Him who died for them.

Every person who comes to the servant should be viewed as a person brought by the Lord of Glory for whom He was crucified. They view the poor and the naked as the person of the crucified and naked Lord Jesus, and the sinner is viewed as the person of Christ who bore the sin of all sinners. Love is martyrdom: "For your sake we are being killed all day long. We are regarded as sheep to be slaughtered. No, in all these things we are more than conquerors through him who loved us" (Romans 8:36-37).

An example in ministry of a loving act is through the agape meal because they encourage love, spiritual trips, camps, prayer meetings, and the divine liturgy. All of these helps the growth of love. Liturgies that are especially for servants and priests together, agape meetings, attention to offerings, attention to church's linen, as spiritual and physical brethren. There is also charity to those in need, whether at home or in life—without preferential giving. The sufferings in the life of the servant for the sake of love are part of the sufferings of Christ, which the servant accepts with joy. "But now I rejoice in my sufferings for you, and I fulfill what is lacking in the afflictions of Christ in my judgment for the sake of his body, which is the church" (Colossians 1:24).

THE MYSTERY OF LOVE & THE CROSS IN MINISTRY

"The servant must lead a life fully immersed in the love of the Crucified One and the power of the Cross."

~ Fr Bishoy Kamel

The Church always requires martyrs of love and martyrs for the unity of the Church. Primarily, love, and secondly, meekness forms the foundations of pastoral ministry within the Church—a characteristic intrinsic to the Church of Christ, whose Head was born in an ox's manger. If this trait is lacking from the priest or servant, Satan can corrupt all their efforts; but, if the priest is humble, he will indeed have the potential to thwart all the powers of Satan.

Once, while the congregation were praying at St. Mark's Church in Šhubrā, our father, Hegumen Mīkhāeĭl Ibrāhīm, approached a member of the congregation, prostrated, and humbly said, "Forgive me." This deed became an embodied lesson of humility in the church now, topping a thousand sermons on humility.

Furthermore, the church instituted the sacrament of washing the feet not as a theatrical performance but as a divine liturgy, bearing the Spirit of God in the waters, allowing the priest to administer the sacrament of washing the people's feet—a profound mystery of humility that highlights the greatness of Christianity.

The most beautiful sight, as stated by Saint Pachomius, is a humble person in whom God dwells. The servant consistently provides from Christ, and not from himself to those whom he serves. He is a devoted man of prayer and supplication, offering them the body and blood of the Lord. As a servant, what is better than that? "What then is Apollos? What is Paul? Servants through whom you believed, as the Lord assigned to each. I planted, Apollos watered, but God gave the growth. So neither he who plants nor he who waters is anything, but only God who gives the growth" (1 Corinthians 3:5-7).

Self-denial is Christ's primary condition for those who follow Him, as the ego forms the root of every affliction in the church. A priest or servant egotistically harbouring anger corrupts the ministry, while a priest who condemns others harms the service. Those who indulge in self-promotion, whether of themselves or their service, bring joy to Satan's heart. Strife and discord emerge as the fruits of pride and egotistical deeds. Therefore, "Blessed are the humble and the poor in spirit, for they will inherit the kingdom of God" (cf. Matthew 5:3-12).

On the cross, we realise the value of the human soul for which Christ died: "By what you eat, do not destroy the one for whom Christ died" (Romans 14:15). We do not look at a person in terms of their position, gender, or social status, but rather for the sake of the One who died for them deems them worthy of the blood of Christ: "Simon, son of Jonah, do you love me? Feed my sheep" (John 21:17). Also, our teacher Paul the Apostle, made the cross the focus and centre of the ministry. He says, "For I decided to know nothing among you except Jesus Christ and Him crucified (1 Corinthians 2:2)" and "For Christ did not send me to baptise but to preach the gospel, and not with words of eloquent wisdom, lest the cross of Christ be emptied of its power" (1 Corinthians 1:17). St Paul considered his ministry and his entire life to revolve around Christ, who was crucified Himself in his place: "O foolish Galatians! Who has bewitched you? It was before your eyes that Jesus Christ was publicly portrayed as crucified" (Galatians 3:1) and "I have been crucified with Christ. It is no longer I who live, but Christ who lives in me" (Galatians 2:20).

Therefore, the Church placed the cross on the iconostasis to be a subject of constant contemplation for the believers throughout their worship. The purpose of the cross, inspiring the priest or servant in their service, is rooted in love and their connection to the One who loved and died for them. The servant views the youth as individuals sent to him by the Lord Jesus

Christ, who was crucified for them. He sees the person of the Lord Jesus in the poor and the naked.

Some individuals believe that the priest's tunic bears two crosses, one on the chest and the other on the back. The first signifies Christ carrying His sufferings and labours, while the second symbolises the priest carrying on his back, along with Jesus Christ, the needs of his people—their pains, sorrows, concerns, and sins. This echoes the words of the Prophet Samuel, "Far be it from me that I should sin against the Lord by ceasing to pray for you, and I will instruct you in the good and the right way" (1 Samuel 12:23).

In the ministry, the servant's duty is to impart to those they serve an understanding of the cross, God's love, His sacrifice, and redemption on every occasion—be it individual or public worship, and baptism (where water symbolises the outpouring from Christ's side on the cross), and the sacrament of Communion. In the ancient tradition of the Church, a wooden cross is placed in baptismal font and water is sprinkled using the cross. In the sacrament of Communion, the sacrifice of divine love is revealed in the slain Lamb who rose for our salvation.

Divine love emanating from the cross is the force that motivates the servant to serve souls. The greater the divine love, the greater the energy for service, as the Apostle says, "For I could wish that I myself were accursed and cut off from Christ for the sake of my brothers, my kinsmen according to the flesh" (Romans 9:3). Our Lord Jesus loved the whole world by way of the cross, for the cross is the ultimate pinnacle of love. The servant must live his entire life fully immersed in the love of the crucified One and the power of the cross.

The cross, therefore, is not the subject of fleeting contemplation for a day, a month, or even a period of time, but rather, divine love in the cross permeates the entire life of the Christian and the servant. Through personal experiences with divine love, the servant could immerse in others the love of Jesus for them and the misery of sin, which can only be erased and redeemed by the blood of the cross—for the sake of Christ's love and the liberating power in Christ that is not felt by anyone outside the circle of the cross. The cross is the power of God for salvation, enabling us to overcome the world, Satan, and the struggles of the body. The cross is the path to freedom and victory, and success.

True freedom is not the freedom of choice, but the freedom to labour with powerful love, rising above the utilitarianism of the world: "And I, when I am lifted up from the earth, will draw all people to myself" (John 12:32)—for there is no liberation outside the circle of the cross.

Repentance

"God does not hold us accountable for our numerous sins, but rather for our failure to repent."

~ Fr Bishoy Kamel

The servant is called to repentance and must continually call people to repentance—a vocation of the prophets in the Old Testament. Repentance is the return of the prodigal son to the embrace of the father and remains the servant's message always, urging every soul to come back to the fold. Repentance is a continuous and complete work, extending from baptism and filling the entirety of the Christian life. Repentance involves the soul's introspection, focusing on oneself rather than looking at others. The moment a person succumbs to criticising others, repentance evades them.

The servant must be a living example of the repentant soul, practicing repentance in their private life, as well as in their fasting, prayers, and love for Christ crucified.

Christianity places a strong emphasis on repentance as a prerequisite for baptism. Without repentance, one cannot fully accept the Holy Spirit and become a child of God. This precedence of repentance is evident in the Book of Acts, where Peter instructed those seeking baptism to repent first, stating, "Repent, and baptise each one in the name of Jesus" (Acts 2:38). This emphasis on repentance may not be as prominent in other religions, where acceptance often precedes repentance. However, foundational principles like repentance are crucial in all religions to maintain their essence and integrity. Without such principles, a religion risks losing its significance.

Repentance stands as the only gateway to the Kingdom of Heaven; no other path can suffice. For instance, it's inconceivable for a Pharisee to deride Christ while simultaneously walking alongside Him. However, repentant sinners can indeed walk in fear with Christ. This underscores the necessity of entering Christianity through the narrow door, as emphasized by Christ's injunction to "take up his cross" to be His disciple.

THE CALL TO FAITH

We carry infinite power in the face of a defeated temporal world despite its strong appearance. This is our faith.

~ Fr Bishoy Kamel

The servant must be a role model in faith, echoing the commandment of the Apostle Paul. Faith is that upon which the servant and those under his care confront the wars posed by the world and Satan, fixing his belief in God's victory for us over the world: "Be of good courage, for I have overcome the world" (John 16:33). The servant must believe that God is with us every day until the end of the age. He must feel a conviction in the magnitude of our victory through Him who loves us and trust that all things work together for good for those who love God. Regardless of the time it takes for the rain to fall, a servant must be patient, firm in faith—the power of the motor propelling the ship of ministry through the tumultuous sea of the world.

Relational Ministry

The ministry of the cross is undertaken by souls who have weaned their emotions and desires from worldly pursuits, instead binding them with the love of God.

~ Fr Bishoy Kamel

The principles and practices of relational ministry were established by Christ Himself. While Christ addressed crowds on numerous occasions, His primary focus was always on individuals. Unfortunately, many servants today overlook this crucial aspect. We often prioritise quantity over quality, seeking validation in large gatherings. However, Christianity has never been about numerical superiority. Such emphasis on numbers typically stems from worldly perspectives, where size equates to strength.

We believe that the power of Christ's life resides within each individual. Take, for example, figures like Abba Antony, whose life represents this power and greatly impacts the Church across generations. Consider also the early days of the Church, when the School of Alexandria emerged under the guidance of Origen during Pope Demetrius' reign. Though they were few in number, their strong structure enabled them to dismantle paganism in Alexandria.

Some people may question the effectiveness of serving in small groups, wondering how a message can reach thousands in such circumstances. They might argue that Christ could have utilised His time more efficiently by ministering to larger crowds during His three years with the twelve disciples. This perspective is flawed!

The element of time holds much significance. Some may perceive the time spent discipling only a few as wasteful, fearing that focusing on quantity and time constraints may jeopardise their service. Consider the Apostle Paul's words, "But when the fullness of time had come, God sent forth his Son, born of woman, born under the law, to redeem those who were under the law, so that we might receive adoption as sons" (Galatians 4:4-5). Was God delayed in His timing?

What about Moses, who spent 40 years seemingly wandering aimlessly in the wilderness before being called by the Lord? Perhaps those years were essential for Moses to reconcile his inner self before receiving his commission. While it may seem like wasted time, Moses wouldn't have been adequately prepared to lead the people without those years of preparation. So, was it better for Moses to lead the people before or after those forty years?

Indeed, while it may seem that Moses spent 40 years in the wilderness without purpose, in the end, victory was achieved. However, the obsession with time and quantity can pose significant threats to the servant, diverting focus from relational ministry. Yet, God has the power to compensate for both time and numbers. He can miraculously provide what is needed in an instant, as when He multiplied five loaves of bread to feed five thousand people through a child.

The saints within the Church may be few in number, but they shine brightly, radiating much light. On the other hand, there may be multitudes who remain in darkness. Therefore, our ministry should be relational and to the few who will become light and salt, living a life in Christ.

Indeed, the impact of relational ministry often exceeds that of a hundred sermons. Consider this: instead of delivering numerous sermons on the words, "If you want to be perfect, go and sell everything you have," wouldn't it be more effective to present a tangible example, like an image of Abba Antony? What about the numerous people who repented upon hearing of Augustine's death, not his sermons?

Allow me to address a crucial aspect that often occupies individuals significantly. The current challenge facing the church lies in the internal disposition of its members. When we encounter our children, whether at university, college, or elsewhere, they often confront difficulties. Instead of facing these challenges head-on, they tend to flee to the safety of the patriarchate or the church, engaging in gossip about their problems. This is not the outcome we strive for. While we certainly desire students who exhibit good Christian behaviour—individuals who bear their cross and follow Christ, responding appropriately to situations and knowing when to remain silent—we also seek those who are inwardly fortified in their faith.

Today, what we truly need are individuals who are complete and confident, not driven by fear. Our aim is not to cultivate superficial appearances but to develop individuals within the church who remain authentic even under pressure. So, how can we effectively engage in relational ministry in light of these considerations?

6.1 Relational Ministry begins at Home

First, let's look into the defining characteristics of relational ministry, which serves as the cornerstone for shaping Christian character. The words of Joshua resonate: "But as for me and my house, we will serve the Lord" (Joshua 24:15). Consider also Timothy's testimony regarding his sincere faith, inherited from his grandmother Lois and his mother Eunice, as recorded in 2 Timothy 1:5. This is not merely a faith preached from a pulpit; rather, it's a faith deeply ingrained through the lived experiences of family members who exemplified a life of devotion.

Such faith is not imparted through lectures or textbooks; it's cultivated through a lifestyle. Christianity is not a theoretical concept confined to pages; rather, it's a way of living, with the home serving as its primary laboratory. Within the home, children witness love for God, prayer, fasting, Scripture reading, compassion towards others, simple living, repentance, faithfulness, gratitude, endurance, and humility. These lived experiences speak louder than a hundred sermons.

When children observe a home where gossip is absent, where love for others prevails, it inspires others to follow suit. Christ himself is saddened by gossip, and a home characterised by genuine love and respect for others is far more genuine than one that preaches love but holds jealousy towards those who excel.

Reflect on Deuteronomy 6:6-10, which instructs, "And these words that I command you today shall be on your heart. You shall teach them diligently to your children." The responsibility to teach falls on the father and mother, as stated, "And shall talk of them when you sit in your house, and when you walk by the way, and when you lie down, and when you rise. You shall bind them as a sign on your hand, and they shall be as frontlets between your eyes. You shall write them on the doorposts of your house and on your gates."

In Jewish tradition, parents would pass down these stories, raise their children in the faith, and adorn their homes with reminders of God's work. A mother who brings her child to church doesn't just drop them off; she stands next to them from a young age, praying with them and sharing Christian stories at bedtime. She embodies the essence of a home church. Similarly, a father who ensures his children's spiritual safety, not only through confession and communion but also by being a beacon of guidance, teaches more through his actions than his words, without scolding or reprimanding.

The home thus becomes a sanctuary where the lives of saints are honoured, and the Bible is a daily presence. Everything in the household points toward Christ.

Families should commemorate the feasts of saints, such as St. Mary on the 21st of each month, or Archangel Michael on the 12th, or the Lord's feasts on the 29th.

The small library in the house is important for each family member who uses it. It should include sections for hymns, prayers, religious writings, and pictures. The house turns into a church, the church in your home. The mother brings her son with her to this church, and he stands beside her while she prays and tells him Christian stories before bedtime. As he sleeps, he is protected by hymns and melodies of the church. The father's role is to reassure the spiritual security of his children, encouraging confession, communion, acts of love, and prayer. He stands as a light and guide in their midst, devoid of any violence or rebuke, teaching more through his actions than his words.

Moreover, relational ministry impels us to take responsibility for our relatives. We have a duty to nurture their spiritual well-being, especially since they are close to us and may be more receptive to our guidance. It's heartening when someone approaches me, saying, "My brother lives in the city, and he feels isolated. Could you please check on him? He's struggling to find motivation to attend church." This demonstrates genuine care and love between siblings. It's not just about making a visit; it's about genuinely caring for their well-being. You can be the catalyst for relational ministry within your family, even if geographical distances separate you.

It is important that neighbours become a spiritual responsibility to the Christian home. I don't mean that they visit all the time, but there needs to be a concern for their spiritual life and delivering spiritual knowledge to them. If they are stubborn people, then there is no need to impose yourself. We are obligated to love like this, and our relational ministry is conducted in love, simplicity, and unforceful.

Relational ministry should also extend to our colleagues. In the Christian life, acts of love should transcend gender or religious boundaries. What the church truly needs today are martyrs of love—individuals who selflessly embody love in all aspects of their lives. It's disheartening to witness individuals, whether a weary child, a fatigued colleague, or someone stifled by their surroundings, succumb to bitterness and resentment. The true test for the church lies in its ability to extend love, both within its community and beyond, coupled with honesty in all its dealings. This means one needs to be tolerant, not return evil by committing evil.

6.2 Controlled Conversations

A characteristic of relational ministry is that we refrain from getting entangled in futile debates, as instructed by the Apostle Timothy (2 Timothy 2). However, we should also be prepared to graciously answer those who inquire about the basis of our hope, with love and patience. There exists a distinction between engaging with someone who seeks understanding with genuine curiosity and someone who merely seeks to bolster their ego through argumentation. Such interactions are driven by pride and a desire for self-importance, often leading to unnecessary conflict. It's best to avoid such discussions, as they only sow discord. Instead, when approached with sincere questions, respond in love and patience.

6.3 Controlled Conduct

Another vital aspect of relational ministry lies in our overall conduct. We must abstain from any behaviour, whether in action or speech, that contradicts Christian principles, as it can undermine our effectiveness in relational ministry. Our aim is to allow the presence of Christ within us to shine before all—not only non-

Christians but also fellow believers. Some individuals may identify as Christians, yet their words and actions do not align with Christian values. Their workplace might even become a breeding ground for gossip and idle chatter. In such situations, the faithful Christian demonstrates patience and resilience. Failing to uphold Christian values tarnishes one's standing and diminishes credibility when sharing the message of Christ. Despite facing initial challenges, the faithful Christian relies on the grace of God to navigate through the trials.

6.4 Visitations

Relational ministry entails the responsibility for servants to visit fellow Christians, ensuring their well-being and spiritual health. It involves fervently praying for distant souls, feeling a sense of accountability towards them, and being willing to visit them, especially in their homes, if the need arises. As St. Paul taught us, "For necessity is laid upon me. Woe to me if I do not preach the gospel!" (1 Corinthians 9:16).

6.5 Within the Parish

At the parish level, relational ministry is deeply ingrained within the fabric of service, through spiritual friendships tended within the church community. I recall watching the Sunday School servants, following their Friday service, gathering together to share a meal at someone's home, engage in Scripture reading, and pray together. I was impelled to reflect on the immense depth of these spiritual friendships compared to the superficial acquaintanceships often found among university colleagues. I realised that the former is characterised by a rich spiritual connection, while the latter often remains at a superficial level of interaction. St Basil had this type of spiritual friendship with St Gregory the Theologian and St John Chrysostom. Spiritual friendship in its simplicity is a participation in the body of Christ—the Church.

6.6 The Grieving

"If there is any comfort from love" (Philippians 2:1).

There are specific groups within the community that the church has a responsibility to care for, and one of these is the grieving individual. Their sorrow is a moving reminder from God, calling us to extend our support and service to them. Unlike those who may distance themselves from God during times of joy, a grieving person is often more open and receptive to the word of God. When we reach out to minister to those who are grieving, our efforts leave a lasting impact. They will remember the compassion and support offered to them by the Church during their time of need.

On this occasion, we have the opportunity to attract many souls to Christ and guide them, shifting their focus to praying liturgies for those who have passed away instead of mourning them. We can direct their eyes to the cross, the Saviour's passion, and the word of God. It is even possible to share in their illness. The intention is not to overwhelm them with excessive courtesy but to assist them in enduring their illness in the spirit of the cross of Christ and the fellowship of His sufferings. Encouraging them to read the Gospel, listen to sermons or melodies, and prayer.

6.7 The Sick

Visiting the sick is a delicate matter that requires careful consideration to avoid overwhelming the individual already burdened with illness. It's crucial to recognise that the sick person may not have the energy to entertain even the slightest inconvenience, let alone a headache. While gestures like gifting chocolates are appreciated, what the sick truly need from us is spiritual support and encouragement. They require conversations that nurture their faith and offer them solace in entrusting their struggles to Christ. If their health permits, reading scripture to them can provide immense comfort. However, the focal point of these interactions should always be the Cross and the understanding of their suffering in the context of Christ's passion.

Encouraging the sick to view their pain as a participation in Christ's suffering invites them to embrace the Cross, to experience it, to feel it, and to love it, knowing that Christ grants grace in abundance. Our role is not to alleviate their physical pain with painkillers—it is our calling to present them with the crucified Christ, the One who shares in their suffering.

6.8 The Widow

Ministering to widows is not just a suggestion but a commandment found in the Epistle of James: "Religion that is pure and undefiled before God the Father is this: to visit orphans and widows in their affliction, and to keep oneself unstained from the world" (James 1:27). It's crucial for widows to feel the loving embrace of the Church as their mother and to find solace and strength in Christ as their ultimate support and comfort. Consider the account of the widow of Nain's son. If her husband were still alive, her son would not have been raised. Through this miracle, Christ demonstrates that He surpasses even the role of a husband. A story like this shows that God is the One who is responsible for the family.

Given the vulnerability widows often experience within society, they deserve special attention and care from the Church. Widows can offer valuable contributions to the community with their unique energy and perspective. Therefore, the pastoral care of widows should be a priority for the Church, recognising both their needs and their potential to enrich the body of believers.

The Sacrament Of

Relational Ministry

Penitents serve as some of the most compelling preachers within the church, and because of them, sinners return to God. ~ *Fr Bishoy Kamel*

7.1 Confession

Concerning the role of the priest, the sacrament of confession is integral to relational ministry. This sacrament involves confessing one's sins on the one hand, and on the other is efforts to develop the penitent's character and foster spiritual growth. The sacrament of confession is sacred because it is one of the seven sacraments of the Church. According to the tradition of some churches, the priest wears his liturgical vestments to perform the sacrament, concluding it before the icon of St. Mary, mother of the Saviour. The repentant feeling that the priest is actively participating in their spiritual journey is a crucial factor in the blessing and success of the sacrament of confession. Hence, the Church selects fathers of confession from priests who possess both experience and a strong foundation in their own lives.

The sacrament of confession holds a significant place within relational ministry, particularly for the priest. Through this sacrament, the priest can impact the lives of the faithful. Confession involves, first and foremost, the confession of sins accompanied by genuine repentance. Additionally, the priest serves to spiritually nurture the repentant, building up their life and uncovering their God-given talents.

Confession is among the seven sacraments of the Church, and in certain traditions, such as the Russian and Greek Orthodox Churches, priests wear their liturgical vestments during the administration of this sacrament, much like in the sacrament of marriage. Even at weddings, priests like Fr. Athanasius from St. Mina's Church, would put on his liturgical vestments to signify the sacred nature of the sacrament being conducted.

During confession of the aforementioned traditions, the priest sits with the repentant before the icon of Saint Mary, Mother of God. The exchange between the repentant and the priest, who shares in their spiritual burden, is integral to the efficacy and success of the sacrament. Therefore, newly ordained priests are not immediately permitted to hear confessions. Instead, they must first mature and gain experience under the guidance of senior clergy before receiving the blessing from the bishop to administer this sacrament. This precaution ensures that the priest's advice is sound and minimizes the risk of errors that could potentially harm the faithful.

The sacrament of confession is a personal encounter with Christ facilitated through the priest. It's essential for the priest to consistently remind the repentant that sins are directed towards God, even if they involve transgressions against fellow human beings. Therefore, it's strongly meaningful for the repentant to initiate their confession with reverent words, such as, "I have sinned against You, O Lord." This declaration establishes from the outset that confession is a direct encounter with God.

Both the repentant and the priest must be mindful of the presence of the Holy Spirit throughout the sacrament, as it is this divine presence that sanctifies the confession. Without this awareness, the sacrament loses its sacred character. Consider someone who approaches confession casually, engaging in idle conversation without recognising the solemnity of the moment. For confession to truly be a sacrament, both the priest and the repentant must approach it with reverence and prayerfulness.

Starting confession with prayer sets the tone for a sacred encounter with God, ensuring that both the repentant and the priest are attuned to the presence of the Holy Spirit and the sanctity of the sacrament.

The repentant must exercise caution against justifying their sins and shifting blame onto others, a tendency that dates back to Adam's response to God. Unfortunately, this tendency persists, particularly among young individuals. For instance, a girl may find herself annoyed by her sister's behaviour at home and, in response, lashes out or uses foul language. Instead of taking responsibility for her actions during confession, she may attempt to shift the blame onto her sister.

By resorting to blame-shifting and excuses, the repentant undermines the essence of confession and forfeits the blessings it offers. When the repentant justifies their actions, they shift from a humble tax collector into a self-righteous Pharisee (Luke 18:9-14). As long as excuses persist, justification before God remains lost. It is only when the repentant refrains from justifying themselves and acknowledges their sins without reservation that justification from the Lord can occur.

7.2 Confession and personal problems

There's a clear distinction between the sacrament of confession and personal issues. It's advisable for confession to commence with prayer, setting the space for a sacred encounter with God. While personal problems may arise during confession, it's essential to prioritise the acknowledgment of sins before God.

Sometimes, especially among younger individuals, personal issues may overshadow the primary purpose of confession. Therefore, it's crucial for the sacrament to begin with prayer and conclude with absolution, allowing the repentant to address their personal concerns afterward. When sins and personal issues become intertwined during confession, there's a risk that the repentant may lose sight of their original intention—to seek forgiveness for their sins. This can lead to confusion and frustration for both the repentant and the priest.

In such instances, it's important for the priest to gently guide the conversation back to the essence of confession, reminding the repentant of the purpose of their presence there. The confession of sins is the primary focus and usually takes only a few minutes. Once absolution is given, the conversation can then extend to address any additional matters outside of confession.

7.3 Applicable Confession

The priest should also recognise the practical dimensions of confession, understanding that negligence in spiritual disciplines like reading the Gospel, prayer, and memorising psalms can also be considered sins. Sin encompasses more than just overt actions like swearing; it also includes the failure to uphold essential spiritual practices, such as service.

As stated in James 4:17, "So whoever knows the right thing to do and fails to do it, for him it is sin." Therefore, the priest considers which specific spiritual services may be appropriate for the repentant, encouraging them to focus on developing spiritual virtues and applying them in their family and work environments. In light of this, the priest also guides the repentant towards a deeper commitment to prayer, a more diligent study of the Bible, and the establishment of a prayer journal.

Through confession, the repentant not only experiences forgiveness but also undergoes a journey towards a more positive outlook on life.

7.4 Clarifying the purpose of confession.

People often think that confession and repentance are the same. There could be a person who has read The Paradise of the Spirit by Bishop Youannis, and come up with pages of sins, as though he went through a checklist, as though they're only ticking boxes (that is a wrong way of reading that book!). You immediately feel that this person is not truly repentant. Fr Mikhail used to say: "The sin that has repentance is seen in someone who feels utter disgust with themselves. Whereas the sin that has no repentance is seen in someone who is completely calm." That is why, when someone comes to me with a checklist of sins, I take the paper off them and put it in my pocket. I ask them to tell me what sin is occupying their mind; what sin is disgusting them, and they want to get rid of. I would tell the person not to bring me a piece of paper, but to bring me their sin.

There are individuals who approach confession as if it were a counselling session. They tend to be talkative and struggle to distinguish between confession and counselling. I don't deny them the opportunity to express themselves, so I ask them to jot down their thoughts in a notebook. They often bring me five pages filled with their words, and I assure them that I'll read it while we're together. Simply scanning the titles brings them solace. However, I still sense emotional turmoil within them. On the other hand, for those who wish to confess and seem psychologically sound, I wonder about their motivations. What do they seek? It remains a mystery to me.

There exists a distinction between repentance and confession. Confession devoid of genuine repentance holds no value. Without repentance, confession becomes an empty ritual. Repentance is the essential precursor to confession, as it involves genuine sorrow for one's sins, a turning away from wrongdoing, and a sincere desire for spiritual transformation. Therefore, the repentant must affirm in their confession that they are truly repentant, by the grace of Christ.

Confession serves as a means for purifying the heart, enabling one to behold God and embark on a life of prayer and communion with our Lord. A touching analogy from the book, The Life of Prayer illustrates this concept beautifully: A person's life resembles a bird's feather, inherently meant to soar. Yet, if even a speck of mud clings to it, the feather remains grounded, unable to fulfill its purpose. Similarly, attempting to fly without first removing what ties us down can lead to injury, like a bird with bound wings attempting to take flight, only to break its limbs.

These parables beautifully illustrate the importance of beginning one's spiritual journey with repentance and confession. Just as the feather must be cleansed of mud to soar freely, and the bird must be freed from its restraints to fly uninhibitedly, so too must we cleanse our hearts through repentance and confession to truly commune with our Lord in prayer and spiritual fellowship.

If there was a person struggling with the lust of the flesh for a long period of time, he might think he is bound by this metaphorical rope. But in fact, he is man engaged in a struggle, and has surrendered to God. Amidst all these conflicts, there lies a crown. Consider the example of Amma Sarah, who led a community of monks and wrestled with the sin of the flesh for 17 years.

Today, our shortcoming is that many young people embark on their spiritual journey with fervour, but as soon as they face difficulties, they may lose hope in God's mercy. However, in spiritual warfare, there is a crown awaiting those who persevere. This does not imply bondage; rather, it signifies one who is a struggler, especially in battles concerning the flesh. Grace comes to aid those who remain faithful in their struggles.

7.5 Spiritual Practices

The priest provides the repentant with practical exercises tailored to their needs, such as memorising psalms or summarising a book of the Bible, which can be both engaging and beneficial. For instance, if someone lacks the virtue of love, I might ask them to summarise the Gospel of John in two pages.

When the repentant returns after a week, they share what they have learned, often realising that they have inadvertently absorbed valuable teachings from the Gospel. These practices not only enrich their spiritual growth but also instil a sense of accomplishment and blessing derived from confession.

I want to remind you that the sacrament of confession is for the recollection of sins. This practice falls outside of confession, while being an offshoot of the sacrament. They are part of the relational ministry offered by the priest to nurture the repentant's spiritual development.

COMMENTS ON CONFESSION

Regular confession purifies the soul, drawing it towards newness of life, particularly when preparing for communion with the body and blood of the Lord.

~ Fr Bishoy Kamel

1. Guiding the repentant to realise that the sin is directed towards God, not towards fellow humans. Therefore, the confession is directed to the Lord Christ. There is, then, no objection to commencing the confession by saying, "I sinned against the Lord Jesus."

2. The repentant must be cautious about justifying sin and placing blame on others who may have contributed to the sin, turning him from the tax collector into the Pharisee (cf. Luke 18:9-14).

3. Differentiating between confession and specific or psychological issues is essential. It is advisable for confession to commence with prayer, conclude with the absolution, and then address any psychological concerns.

4. The priest should focus on the aspects of faith during confession, including prayer, fasting, Scripture memorisation, consistent Bible study, and the use of a meditation journal. He should inquire about the individual's service to God within the realms of family, work, and acts of love, while emphasising the cultivation of virtues. The ultimate aim of confession is repentance, as confession devoid of repentance holds no value.

5. One of the objectives of confession is the attainment of a pure heart and a life characterized by prayer. Confession

is not an end in itself but rather a means to achieve a heart purified enough to behold God.

6. Confession serves as a platform for the priest to identify talents within the church, nurture them, and guide individuals to utilize their gifts. Someone with leadership talent might be encouraged to serve in Sunday schools, while a person with a passion for others could engage in individual service. Another with a talent for hidden social service may be directed towards aiding the needy, and someone inclined towards manual service could find a niche there. Another individual might be inspired to read and write more. This illustrates that confession is an individualised process at its highest level, and the priest provides tailored guidance to each repentant. This guidance may involve activities such as memorising a specific psalm, training in the Agpia prayer, summarising a book from the Gospel, engaging in personalised Bible study, reflecting on the significance of the cross, and contemplating the Lord's Prayer, "Our Father who art in heaven."

7. Confession can encounter challenges, particularly when there is a large number of repentants. To address this, specific days can be designated for confession for young men and women, as well as for families. Given the commonality of sins and weaknesses, group confession

can be considered. In this format, repentants gather for a session where a general discussion covers various types of sins and strategies for overcoming them. The priest then provides the appropriate training for each sin, followed by individual confession with the priest praying for and addressing each person in turn.

8. One issue faced by young women in confession is occasional hesitation or embarrassment in listing certain youthful sins. In such cases, the priest can quickly pass through those topics, being careful not to discuss sins that the repentant may not be familiar with. Very often do we see young girls not wanting to confess because of this reason. Our role as servants is to move their heart toward repentance. Eventually, when the young girl visits the priest, she will become exposed to the wisdom and guidance of the Church.

9. At times, confession can lead to an attachment to the priest, and this is a significant aspect for the priest to be mindful of while administering the sacrament.

Ministry & Discipleship

'Lord Jesus, I do not seek a particular cross, but the one chosen by Your will for me. I do not seek to give away my ministry, but ask to be used by You in it.

~ Fr Bishoy Kamel

Twelve disciples were commissioned by the Lord Jesus Christ. This was mentioned in the sixth chapter of the Gospel of our teacher Mark, the tenth chapter of the Gospel of our teacher Matthew, and the ninth chapter of the Gospel of our teacher Luke. The three Gospels talked about Christ's mission to the 12 disciples. Our teacher Luke also spoke about Christ's mission to the 72 apostles.

When we read these chapters, we realise a very important point: For Christ, service was not just that He came to preach and teach people, but to make disciples. That is why every Christian was called a disciple of Christ. He said, "Whoever wants to be my disciple" (Matthew 16:24; Mark 8:34; Luke 9:23). Then he began by giving us the conditions for discipleship. It remains clear from Christ's words that it is He who makes disciples.

Some might find it surprising that Christ dedicated three years of service to only twelve individuals. However, it's essential to note that there were also another seventy disciples. Out of the twelve, one turned out corrupt—Judas.

Christ's practical approach to ministry is evident. He provided clear guidelines that we, as His followers, are not entitled to alter or devise anew. Christianity fundamentally embodies discipleship, and Christ deemed it necessary to educate His followers accordingly. Christianity is discipleship, and Christ needed to educate His disciples. One might say that this is a waste of time, but Christ insists that this is the way. Christianity is the way of life, and it is transferred from one person to another. Christianity isn't merely about preaching or engaging in propagandist activities. Christianity is about the individual Christian person, discipled by Christ through the Holy Spirit.

When we read about what it means to be a Christian in the book of Acts, we find that the later disciples were referred to as Christians, while the earlier ones were called disciples. All Christians are called to be disciples. Central to discipleship is the concept of mentorship or guidance from one person to another. For example, when we come to support a young child, we are actually becoming his sponsor. The significance of sponsorship may be underestimated in modern times, particularly in the context of baptismal rites.

While today's sponsors often participate in the baptism ceremony and hold the child during the renunciation of Satan, historically, sponsorship carried a deeper meaning within the church community. In the past, every member of the church was expected to have a sponsor, highlighting the communal aspect of spiritual support and guidance within the Christian faith.

The term "sponsor" carries the connotation of being a representative. Think of parable of the talents. Our Lord was the one who asked, "How many talents do you have in your hand?" (Cf. Matthew 25:14-30; Luke 19:12-28). While it's true that those entrusted with five talents may receive a significant reward, it's essential to recognise that this reward is contingent upon diligent effort and the responsible stewardship of those talents. Rather than comparing ourselves to others and questioning why some seem to have been given more talents than us, we should focus on faithfully utilising the talents entrusted to us. It's worth noting that those who have been given more talents will be held to a higher level of accountability.

The 72 apostles were not only disciples of Christ but also elevated to the role of apostleship, a progression beyond mere discipleship. However, note that Christ spent a significant amount of time with them, a period spanning three years, during which they were deeply immersed in His teachings and guidance. This period of discipleship is also mirrored in the actions of the Apostle Paul. In Ephesus, faced with opposition from the local community, Paul chose to invest his time in discipling others. He spent three years teaching and mentoring individuals at a school associated with a figure named Tyrannus.

Allow me to share an encounter I had while traveling last summer. During a stop at a restaurant, I met a young man named Richard, who shared his remarkable journey with us. Originally Christian, Richard had converted to Islam, and we engaged in a conversation about his faith transition. We asked him what he knew about Islam. He said, "I know a lot of things very well. I will recite to you al-Fatihah and I will recite to you a Surah." He was alternating between English and Arabic recitations. We were surprised and asked him, "How did you learn all of that?" Richard told us that he was a teaching assistant student here at the Faculty of Science at Alexandria University, and he is going to study for a doctorate at the University of Southern California. He was there studying in the morning; he dedicated his afternoons to mentoring others. Remarkably, for two years, he discipled 14 families!

I believe that the world has learned a lot about discipleship from Christianity. Nowadays, we might see the disciple bore as one who carries the bag for the bishop or the patriarch. However, throughout the history of the Church, we have witnessed instances where patriarchs entrusted their disciples with their deepest secrets and teachings, viewing them as successors who had imbibed from their own cup.

Our Lord Jesus Christ was the first to emphasise the importance of discipleship as an integral aspect of one's spiritual education. There are two fundamental aspects to Christ-centred discipleship. Firstly, as a disciple of Christ, one must adhere to His teachings, exemplified by denying oneself, taking up the cross, and following Him. Secondly, discipleship extends beyond personal devotion to Christ; it involves nurturing and guiding others in their own faith journey. Whether you have one disciple or several, you must be an active person in the Christian life whose life embodies service. This is what it means to be a disciple of Christ, and to make disciples in Christ.

By adopting this approach, your disciples in Christ will also be inspired and empowered to make their own disciples. It's akin to Christ sitting with His disciples, instructing them, and then sending them forth into the world. Picture Christ sitting with them and saying, "Okay, now go." They might be thinking, "What? Already?" He tells them to go out into the field, taking on the practical educational model where disciples are challenged to apply their learning in real-life scenarios.

Discipleship is not confined to theoretical knowledge; it requires disciples to live out their faith and share it with others. This approach to discipleship has influenced various fields, including social services and nursing, where the emphasis on serving others is deeply rooted in Christian principles.

These practices originated within the confines of monasteries and Christian communities. In the early days, monks and nuns who possessed nursing skills would establish small hospitals within their monastic communities, where the sick would seek care. Similarly, monks and nuns would attend to the needs of their elders, thus laying the foundation for what would later evolve into the nursing profession. Over time, nursing expanded beyond the confines of monasteries and became a widespread practice accessible to all, regardless of religious affiliation.

With the departure from Christ-centred discipleship in nursing, there has been a noticeable decline in the sincerity of gentleness and compassion traditionally associated with the profession. Nursing has become more routinized, lacking the personal touch and spiritual grounding it once had.

A similar trend can be observed in social services. While individuals may hold titles such as social supervisor or social worker, the essence of compassionate service often seems to be lost. Rather than embodying the spirit of discipleship and serving others with gentleness and wisdom, these roles have become bureaucratic and focused solely on administrative tasks. In contrast, the early Christian church illustrated the principles of discipleship in its approach to social services. When faced with challenges such as the distribution of food among the growing number of disciples (Christians), the church appointed seven deacons filled with wisdom and the Holy Spirit to manage their issues.

Consider Stephen, who was appointed for the distribution of food and supplies. Filled with wisdom and the Holy Spirit, Stephen was discipled at the hands of the apostles. Following the pattern set by Jesus, who sent out His disciples on practical missions for training, they would return and report to Him all they had accomplished and taught. This mirrors Mark's account: "The apostles returned to Jesus and told Him all that they had done and taught" (Mark 6:30). Just as the disciples shared with Jesus, we can envision ourselves at day's end, gathering with Him to discuss our experiences and insights. "And he said to them, 'Come away by yourselves to a desolate place and rest a while.' For many were coming and going, and they had no leisure even to eat" (Mark 6:31). Here, Jesus acknowledges the importance of rest and reflection amid the demands of ministry.

Here, I envision a vivid scene of Christ seated with His twelve disciples gathered around Him. Christ initiates their mission, urging them to action with a simple command, "Let's go." The disciples respond eagerly, seeking guidance on their course of action. Christ provides them with specific instructions, detailing not only what to say but also practical steps to take, including what provisions to bring and preparations to make. With their instructions clear, they embark on their mission and serve.

Upon their return, the disciples eagerly recounted their experiences to Christ, sharing everything they had done during their time away. Sensing their excitement, Christ invites them to a quiet place for reflection and accountability, where they can assess the effectiveness of their ministry. This scenario prompts us to consider our own role as servants of God and the accountability we hold in our ministries. At the end of each day, we present our accounts to God, detailing our actions. However, there is a cautionary story embedded in the Gospel narrative, as seen in the account of the 72 disciples in Luke 10:17. These disciples returned from their mission filled with joy, boasting about their ability to cast out demons in Jesus' name. Yet, Christ gently redirects their focus, reminding them that true cause for rejoicing lies not in exorcising demons but in the assurance of their names being recorded in the book of the Kingdom of Heaven. Christ corrected their misinterpretation of ministry.

Christ instructed them to approach their service with calmness, acknowledging that challenges would arise. He advised them to enter every house, accepting whatever was offered to them, and to extend peace to each household with gentleness and composure. Thus, ministry commences with love and fosters personal relationships. Should they encounter a receptive individual, peace would reside in that place. If they faced rejection, they were not to take offense but to express gratitude for the hospitality offered and symbolically shake off the dust from their feet. In this act, Christ conveyed not a curse upon the house but a gesture of disengagement, signifying that even the dust clinging to their feet would not trouble the household further.

For this reason, Christianity never instructs us to succumb to frustration. On the contrary, our message embodies love, simplicity, peace, inner strength, and the calm proclamation of our Lord's teachings. Discipleship compels a feeling of divine commission and the guidance of the Holy Spirit, to serve as fellow labourers in the Kingdom of our Lord Jesus Christ.

Christ's commandment, "Go and make disciples of all nations," stresses action and movement in ministry. The term "Go" signifies active engagement, urging disciples to go out and serve others. It's not solely about preaching, but a servant will make disciples out of his own children!

Discipleship involves a continuous process where one person mentors and teaches another. Unlike passive listening to sermons, discipleship entails providing ongoing lessons and guidance, leading individuals to become disciplined followers of Christ. It's through discipleship that individuals receive the Spirit of Christ and grow in their faith.

Anyone aspiring to disciple others must first be open to being discipled themselves. Discipleship is a central aspect of the Church's mission, leading the entire body of believers to become disciples of Christ. Every Christian is called to both receive discipleship and impart it to others. This mirrors Christ's own ministry on earth, where He mentored the twelve apostles, then extended His guidance to 72 others. Even amidst His public ministry, Christ prioritised the nurturing and teaching of His disciples. Examples abound, such as His transfiguration before Peter, James, and John on Mt. Tabor, His insightful response to the disciples' question about greatness, and His personal encounter with Thomas to dispel doubt. These instances show Christ's intimate and individualised approach to discipleship.

A church that actively engages in disciple-making can be likened to a "birth-giver" of Christians. However, a church that merely delivers sermons without fostering discipleship will not bear spiritual fruit and may have a superficial congregation.

It is crucial for servants or priests to pray for each person they serve, seeking to discern their unique talents and how they can best contribute to the church's mission. A successful ministry involves not only preaching but also nurturing and guiding individuals to become disciples who, in turn, make disciples.

To fulfill the commandment to make disciples of "all nations," there are no restrictions on where discipleship can occur. As St. Paul advised, "be ready in season and out of season" (2 Timothy 4:2). We must be prepared at all times, ready to engage in disciple-making regardless of the circumstances. This means that we should never deem any situation as unsuitable for disciple-making. Whether in our workplaces, through preaching, or by demonstrating love to others, the opportunity to disciple others is ever-present. Retreating into introversion or isolation is akin to shirking our responsibility to engage in ministry. Discipleship is a condition of being Christ's follower.

Discipleship entails following the example of Christ, which includes bearing our own crosses as He did. As long as Christ carries His cross, we too must walk in His footsteps and carry our own crosses.

To engage in discipleship effectively, one needs a teacher, a guide, and access to the Holy Bible. The Holy Spirit is our interpreter and teacher when studying the Scriptures. Continuous study of the Bible is essential for discipleship, as there is no other source of knowledge in this world that can compare to the wisdom found within its pages.

Obedience to Christ and His commandments is central to discipleship.

Pastoral Love

In The Church

Pastoral ministry in the Church is a gift of the Holy Spirit bestowed upon priests, deacons, and Sunday school ministers. Entrusted with the responsibility to emulate the life of Christ within the Church, they are called to practice love, purity, humility, self-denial, and oneness of spirit in their behaviour. Through their conduct, they are to glow with the rational aroma and beautiful image of Christ.

These ministers are tasked with teaching the work of Christ by the rebirth of souls through baptism, nurturing them with untainted milk drawn from the breath of the Gospel and the teachings of the Church. They must discover different talents in themselves and those they serve and seek to develop them.

Diligently striving for the growth of love in the church is imperative, because "he who does not love does not know God" (1 John 4:8). They endeavour to attract lost souls, proclaiming to them the extraordinary love of Christ for repentant sinner. In every sermon and teaching, they echo the call to repentance, viewing it as a natural extension of baptism, all while exuding a compassionate, fatherly love.

These servants should strive to show the image of the cross in the lives of each of Christ's flock. The cross is a declaration of God's love and the power of victory. All who believe this become disciples of Christ, denying themselves, carrying the cross, and following him. Their relationships with the cross changes into a life of love and prayer. They strive to do this with all diligence so that the church transforms into a castle of prayer and love.

They teach the word of the Gospel in their lives and in their meditations, and they meditate on it with their flock day and night. They adhere to the Church's festivities, saints' lives, her history, fasting, and worship. For she is the barn whereby the sheep enter, are saved, and find pasture.

The foundation of every ministry is love. Love is the first relationship of the Church of Christ, and it is the nerve that connects each member of the Church. Today, love requires martyrs without shedding blood who are no less powerful than martyrs of blood. The purpose of the commandment is love: "love one another earnestly from a pure heart" (1 Peter 1:22).

Love must get rid of hypocrisy, so we should not be two-faced, speaking with honest words within our narrow society's broad communities.

Christ's Authority Conquers Evil Against The Church

My Lord Jesus, grant me understanding and awareness of the power of Your cross. Let me feel, amidst the tribulations of the world and its contrary principles, that I am not vanquished but triumphant through the might of Your cross.

~ Fr Bishoy Kamel

The authority bestowed upon the disciples by Christ was not solely for the purpose of exorcising demons, although that was a significant aspect of their ministry. Rather, it encompassed a broader mandate against the forces of darkness, particularly Satan himself. While casting out demons was part of their mission, Satan's resistance to Christ's ministry on earth extended far beyond mere demon possession. Therefore, Christ empowered them to confront Satan directly, recognising that his opposition to the Church would manifest in various forms. It's essential to understand that any opposition to the message of Christ ultimately originates from Satan. Thus, when encountering challenges from the world, it's crucial to stand firm, knowing that these adversities are orchestrated by the enemy of good.

Satan's plans often involve undermining the authority of Christ and His Church, seeking to disrupt the work of God and hinder the spread of His message. One example of this is when a demon-possessed woman was brought to the Church of St. Mary in Cleopatra, Alexandria while it was being built. As I prayed for her deliverance, her voice changed, and the demon spoke through her. When questioned about why it was inhabiting the woman, the demon claimed that she had offered it a sacrifice. So I told him, "What does you mean by offering you a sacrifice?" I didn't understand. The demon said, "You're telling me that you don't understand, O priest? Do you not offer sacrifices on this altar?"

Satan knows that there is a sacrifice being offered on this altar. The world is agitated. Satan is agitating the world because he knows that the altar of God is here. Do not worry about Satan's frenzy. Christ gave the disciples authority over Satan. When they said to Him, "Demons are cast out for us in Your name." He said to them, "I have given you the power to trample over serpents and scorpions, and over all the power of the enemy."

Understand that the enmity between the Church and the world is fundamentally a battle between Christ and Satan. Consider the example of Herod: despite the innocence of the infant Christ born in a humble manger, Herod felt threatened. It was Satan who whispered into Herod's ear while he slept, planting the idea that this child posed a threat to his reign. Consequently, Herod ordered the massacre of innocent children. Satan played with his mind.

My brothers and sisters, it is Satan who continues to incite hostility against God's children in the world today. Christ himself referred to Satan as an "unclean spirit," emphasizing the spiritual nature of this conflict.

There is a pressing need for the Church to remain steadfast in the face of challenging times. The Church must strengthen the faith of its children so that they become strong and resilient against the currents of the world. Like a mother guiding her child to walk and then allowing them to walk alone, the church must watch over be vigilant over her children's sacrifice of faith, offering them Christ so that they may live by Him— Christ who conquered the world. The Church then lets them go out into the world with Christ embedded in their lives, faithfully confident that the One who is in them is mightier than the one who is in the world.

To tackle this, we must learn the foundations of our Orthodox faith. The foremost is the constant presence of God in our lives. Our faith is different from any other faith. It is not merely in acknowledging the power, greatness, and authority of God, and that the heavens speak of His glory, or the ark revealing the work of His hands. Rather, our faith is rooted in the fact that we are temples of the Holy Spirit (1 Corinthians 6:19). We carry Christ in our lives, and the Church believes that Christ will never leave us. Even if a person renounces their faith and later repents the Church does not baptise them again, but only calls on them to repent.

Secondly, we continually partake of the body and blood of the Lord, practicing death to the world and repentance. We pray and eat the body of the Lord, knowing that we will live eternally in Him. This faith transforms us to be more than ourselves. It means that there is an infinite divine augmentation to our finite humanity. We believe that God united with our nature by taking what is ours and giving us what is His, and we believe in the one incarnate nature of Christ after uniting with the body of our humanity. This faith leads us to affirm: "Whoever believes in Me will also do the works that I do; and greater works than these will he do" (John 14:12).

The infinite augmentation of God into our weak nature gives the Christian person the ability to enter into infinitudes and perform works, possible by God's own infinitude.

Priestly Fatherhood

The priest[1] (πρεσβύτερος, presbuteros), meaning an intercessor, prays for his people in the sacrifice of the liturgy and in his prayers: "Far be it from me that I should sin against the Lord by ceasing to pray for you." (1 Samuel 12:23).

Fatherhood is a distinctive characteristic of the priest, which he takes from the person of the Heavenly Father. Our relationship as Christians with God is a relationship of sonship. It seems to me that the main work of Christ is that he declares to us the nature of God as Father. He gave us the Holy Spirit who cries within us, saying: Our Father in Heaven. In Christ, I can therefore call God "My Father."

Fatherhood is revealed to us by God through various teachings, such as the parable of the prodigal son, the Lord's Prayer, and the subsequent parable in Luke 11. In this passage, Jesus asks, "What father among you, if his son asks for a fish, will instead of a fish give him a serpent; or if he asks for an egg, will give him a scorpion? If you then, who are evil, know how to give good gifts to your children, how much more will the heavenly Father give the Holy Spirit to those who

---

1 Originally titled, "Fatherhood," was a lecture Fr Bishoy delivered at the theological college.

ask Him!" (Luke 11:11-13) This illustrates the loving and giving nature of God as a Father, who desires to provide good things to His children, especially the gift of the Holy Spirit to those who seek Him.

As a father, the priest experiences the emotions of his congregation with a paternal love. This love isn't indulgent or materialistic, but rather it is focused on the spiritual well-being and salvation of his flock. True fatherhood is characterised by a balance of tenderness and firmness, with the ultimate aim of guiding souls towards spiritual growth and salvation.

The Apostle Paul beautifully expressed this sentiment in Galatians 4:19: "My little children, for whom I am again in the anguish of childbirth until Christ is formed in you!" Have you ever witnessed such profound fatherhood? It illustrates that true fatherhood isn't about material concerns but about nurturing Christ-like qualities in others. When a father witnesses Christ's presence in all his children, it brings him immense joy.

Fatherhood calls for a life of purity, as the Apostle Paul advised Timothy, "Let no one despise you for your youth, but set the believers an example in speech, in conduct, in love, in faith, in purity" (1 Timothy 4:12).

The servant's faith is akin to engaging in a battle with the world and the devil on behalf of those they serve. The servant or priest acts as a commander in this spiritual warfare. If their own faith is weak, how can they effectively support those who struggle alongside them? It's the duty of the servant to elevate the faith of those they serve.

I've witnessed this in those I minister to. I guide them to a point where they are confident that Christ has triumphed over the world. Their faith grows to a level where they give no attention to the world's problems and troubles. It's reminiscent of the courage displayed by the three young men in the fiery furnace, as we feel and believe that God is with us always, even unto the end of time. This confidence remains accessible to every soul in the church, reminding us that God is with us through every trial.

As role models for believers, fathers manifest love, spirit, faith, and purity. While we all have weaknesses, the essence of our church is one of holiness and purity. This implies that anyone entering the church is actively pursuing a life in communion with Christ. As St. Paul emphasized, "For without holiness, no one will be able to see the Lord" (Hebrews 12:14). When this image of holiness is distorted within the church, it undermines everything. A stumble in this regard is profoundly serious, as it undermines the very purpose for which individuals revere the house of our Lord.

The Book of the Song of Songs portrays the church as a collective community, likening it to a breathtaking sight: "Who is this who looks down like the dawn, beautiful as the moon, bright as the sun, awesome as an army with banners?" (Song of Songs 6:10). Similarly, in the Liturgy, we express the transformative work of God in our lives, affirming that He purifies us by His Holy Spirit.

The pursuit of holiness is the ultimate aim for every Christian, a journey that the priest not only models but also guides and fosters in others. In the pursuit toward holiness, the soul engages with the Holy Spirit, navigating spiritual struggles, and faithfully adhering to practices like fasting and prayer. What sets Christianity apart is its emphasis on inner transformation rather than mere external rituals or appearances. Christ instituted the Church to be a holy sanctuary where the inner life of individuals is nurtured and cherished above all else.

Are you familiar with the tale of the girl who was coerced into using magic against St. George? As she rode behind him on horseback, she confessed, "They brought me to ensnare you with magic and deceit, but your purity has enchanted me far more effectively."

Consider the words of the Apostle Paul: "Do you not know that your body is a temple of the Holy Spirit within you, whom you have from God? You are not your own, for you were bought with a price. So glorify God in your body" (1 Corinthians 6:19-20). Likewise, James writes, "Or do you suppose it is to no purpose that the Scripture says, 'He yearns jealously over the spirit that he has made to dwell in us'?" (James 4:5).

Youth Ministry And Today's Challenges

The servant is someone whose dirty feet Jesus washed and continues to wash every day. Because of this, he walks alongside Jesus wholeheartedly, seeking to cleanse the filth from everyone. He carries with him a heartfelt conviction that Jesus is still washing his feet.

~ Fr Bishoy Kamel

Peoples outlook on the current era varies widely. Some see no crises, while others liken the world to Sodom and Gomorrah. However, Christian life remains possible amidst either of these perspectives and challenges, as God's grace abounds even in the face of sin (Romans 5:20).

Modern developments have brought about significant changes, even in warfare, with the emergence of technology and electronic warfare. From the West, where scientific and technological advancements are prevalent but spiritual heritage is lacking, new problems have emerged. Our challenge lies in not only recognising these issues but also in avoiding the hasty adoption of Western mistakes.

Here, we outline four contemporary problems that demand our attention and response guided by the Spirit of God.

12.1 The Challenge of Atheism

Atheism poses a significant challenge worldwide, particularly in regions experiencing rapid scientific advancements. This progress has led many to embrace a form of modern atheism, rejecting traditional beliefs in favour of human-made ideologies and materialistic theories. In countries like France, once considered Christian strongholds, the number of practicing Christians has dwindled compared to the overall population, with urban areas experiencing greater spiritual detachment than rural communities.

The allure of modernity and scientific advancement has fuelled waves of atheism, especially among youth and children, sparking discussions and doubts about matters of faith.

However, scientific progress itself cannot be blamed for the rise of atheism. Atheism is a deeply personal and subjective issue rooted in individuals' attachment to certain deviant behaviours that trouble their conscience. Often, atheism serves as a means to suppress the inner voice of conscience that urges repentance. According to Saint Augustine, there are no genuine atheists; atheism is a fabricated concept. In truth, we are all believers at our core, yearning for the solace found only in the embrace of God. Deep within us lies an innate recognition of God and a longing for peace in His hands.

In scientifically and economically advanced societies, the significance of faith for the human soul becomes increasingly apparent. Despite remarkable progress, there is a continual rise in psychological illnesses and neurological disorders. There is a spiritual and psychological void within humanity that can only be filled by Christ. The profound secret behind the spiritual and psychological well-being of the human soul lies in the presence of the Lord in our lives. Neither material possessions nor relationships can provide the deep heavenly peace that Christ offers, for He is our ultimate "source of peace" (Ephesians 2:14).

The Church must prepare to study these contemporary trends, analysing their origins and underlying causes. It's essential to provide today's youth with robust Christian guidance and a solid foundation in the Gospel. Our youth need to be grounded in the truth, illuminated by the Holy Spirit, and nourished by the Word of God. Throughout history, the Church has confronted and withstood various challenges, adapting to absorb new ideas while remaining faithful to its core beliefs. Just as figures like Origen engaged with pagan philosophies to defend Christianity, we must mobilise both intellectually and spiritually to counter modern ideologies and attacks on fundamental Christian faith that aim to separate the Holy Trinity, attack the divinity of Christ, and question His incarnation and holy crucifixion. We face a spiritual battle, and it's imperative to equip our youth to withstand these challenges and remain steadfast in their faith.

12.2 The Problem of Anxiety

Secondly, we face the widespread problem of anxiety in the twentieth century. This century has brought about a surge in physiological disorders like hypertension, angina, and ulcers, stemming from chronic nervous exhaustion and fear. From a young age, individuals are plagued by anxiety, navigating through a relentless cycle of exams, educational milestones, career aspirations, and family planning. The prospect of emigration for better opportunities or securing appointments in distant lands adds to this burden. Consequently, life has become a succession of apprehensions and uncertainties. Parents worry about their children's futures, while mothers fear societal deviations impacting their daughters, and the once-stable fabric of society is now fraught with instability.

What's the antidote? Nothing but faith! Fear is merely the absence of faith. Faith is instilled in children from a young age, nurtured at home, cultivated in the church environment, and braced through life experiences. Our forebears lived with modest means, living out the Apostle Paul's teaching: "But if we have food and clothing, with these we will be content" (1 Timothy 6:8). They maintained an attitude of gratitude towards God in all circumstances, even amidst persecution and hardship!

I once met an individual who had migrated overseas and amassed great wealth, yet lived in constant fear of losing it, theft, illness, or sudden death! Fear is a dreadful emotion that corrodes the soul, and our sole weapon against it is faith in Christ. Faith empowered Joseph in Potiphar's house, assured him of God's presence in the house; it emboldened Daniel in the lion's den, and sustained Nehemiah in rebuilding Jerusalem's walls amid adversity and despair.

Our excessive grumbling and complaints in the presence of our children may encourage a generation marked by weakness and fear. What we truly need today is to heed the voice of the Lord: "Take heart; it is I, do not be afraid" (Mark 6:50). Through faith, we conquer anxiety and oust fear, even if our faith in Christ invites mockery or reproach. Our lively faith serves as a tangible testament to the authenticity of the Christian journey and the inherent need of the human soul for it.

When we rely solely on calculations, we hinder God's work, leading to His withdrawal from our midst. However, when we witness the mighty hand of God at work, as the Church and the Gospel consistently do, miracles unfold. Philip, too, questioned the feasibility of feeding the multitude with inadequate resources, yet the Lord's faithful provision turned scarcity into abundance. Our Church is endowed with a wealth of faith, a heritage we mustn't squander due to our frailties. Let us impart this spiritual arsenal to our children, enabling them to confront adversity, engage in the Lord's battles, and overcome fear and anxiety. May we instil in them the spirit of contentment, gratitude, and firm trust in the loving God, capable of all things.

12.3 Empathy Depravation

It's often said that Egyptians are deeply emotional, yet globally, compassion seems to be waning. Even mothers, traditionally epitomising tenderness, find themselves emotionally drained amidst the pressures of modern life. Juggling work from dawn to dusk, many children are left in daycare, missing out on the warmth and affection they crave. A moving observation captures the modern dilemma: Children are being raised more by appliances than by mothers.

The current generation is experiencing a severe lack of affection, to the extent that experts advise mothers who resort to formula milk to still hold their children close and attempt breastfeeding. This emotional deprivation lies at the root of many contemporary issues. Girls, especially, yearn for affection and readily respond to any display of kindness, even from those outside their religious community. It's not uncommon to see a girl prefer the attention of a socially inferior young man over the paternal comforts of her own home. When parents are preoccupied with work and neglect to provide emotional nourishment, they sow the seeds of rebellion and discord in their children.

The family serves as a child's initial classroom, but the discord within many Christian households inhibits the development of a peaceful and balanced youth. As parents, we transmit our faith to our children, recalling the Apostle Paul's guidance to Timothy: "I am reminded of your sincere faith, a faith that dwelt first in your grandmother Lois and your mother Eunice and now, I am sure, dwells in you as well" (2 Timothy 1:5). A family that regularly convenes around the family's prayer altar and delves into the teachings of the Holy Gospel fosters for the youth an environment of internal serenity, spiritual contentment, and a love for holiness.

I met an unemployed mother who attempted to run a small daycare from her home but soon shut it down. The reason was out of concern for her own children, fearing that the other children were troubled and faced difficulties, often stemming from being the offspring of divorced parents (as divorce rates abroad have soared to over 80%). Our critical need is for nurturing families that instil love in their children, eradicating selfishness from their hearts.

12.4 Life in the Fast Lane

Modern civilization has stripped individuals of the necessary free time to calm themselves, pray, read, and connect with family and friends in healthy Christian love. There are no longer moments for solitude each day or opportunities for weekly retreats to realign with

Christ, address weaknesses and sins, find solace in the Lord, and intercede for others. Despite advancements in technology, individuals remain in a constant state of rush, engrossed in work and material pursuits, leading to extreme exhaustion.

The youth must take a firm stand for the path of Christ, and the Church must unequivocally address the allure of worldly distractions. I once met a young man abroad who expressed his hatred for sin, yet admitted feeling weary of attending church regularly. Unless we take a decisive stance and call our youth to a deeper, authentic Christian life, we'll continue drifting in the same direction. Today's youth grapple with anxiety and confusion, yearning for the consoling embrace of Christ. In Him, we find fulfillment, conquer evil, and radiate peace. The era's challenges aren't insurmountable; rather, it's the shallow commitment of Christ's followers that poses the real issue. If they rooted themselves deeply in faith, they'd become guiding lights for the lost youth of our time.

MISCELLANEOUS QUOTES

ON MINISTRY

The Cross of Ministry

1. When the heart serves others for the sake of the Lord Jesus, His image is imprinted upon it, and it becomes illuminated by His light.

2. The one who rises with Christ on the cross must have experienced the power of being dead to the world, the power of the resurrection, and ultimately, the power of ascending to heaven. With this power, one descends into the world to serve, lifting its children to greater heights.

3. The servant's task in service is to impart to others the message of the Cross, God's love, and His sacrifice.

4. The servant must lift the faith of those he serves to the point where they are assured that Christ has conquered the world. Their faith should transcend the world's challenges and difficulties, believing firmly that God is with us always, until the end of time.

5. Meekness is an essential quality of the Church of Christ, whose leader was born in a humble cow's manger. Should this attribute be absent from the priest or servant, Satan will corrupt their efforts.

6. Shepherds turn their relationship with the cross into a life of love and prayer. They diligently strive for this until the church becomes a fortress of prayer.

7. The shepherd or servant is a martyr of love, fuelled by the strength derived from Christ's love on the cross. He embraces love and shuns hatred, for love—meaning God—never fails.

8. Love is the tie that binds the shepherd to his flock.

9. The angry priest and servant spoil the ministry.

10. The priest and servant who loves to condemn others corrupts the ministry.

11. The priest or servant who seeks personal glory through their ministry delights Satan's heart.

12. The one who lives a life faithful to Christ bears His image and aroma, spreading it everywhere.

13. If you possess a talent but hold contempt for others, God will withdraw it from you.

14. Ministry is akin to unearthing springs of water in the lives of those being served, allowing the continual current of the spirit to permeate their souls.

15. Ministry is not about adding something new to those being served, but rather about revealing the hidden springs within them.

16. Ministry involves clearing away the dust and uncovering the springs—the wellsprings of prayer and the continual kindling of love for the crucified Jesus, the sources of the Holy Spirit's gifts, and channelling these talents to edify the body of the church—the sources of the Word of God and discovering the richness of the Gospel in our lives.

17. Ministry is to help the young person discover the sources of the richness of the soul and the power of faith within him so that one can face the world in the spirit of prayer and the spirit of the Gospel.

18. Every Ministry should stress the blessings of baptism and the gift of new life. It should involve discussions about repentance, digging into the springs of spiritual renewal. Each ministry should conclude with an internal stirring—a prayerful movement of repentance, love, service, and tears—that emanates from within.

19. Ministry is an ongoing internal formation. The spirit continually draws from the riches of Christ and bestows them upon the church each day.

20. Continuous labour is inherent to God's nature. "My Father is working until now, and I am working also"

(John 5:17). This labour persists in the lives of the saints even after they depart from this world.

21. Be careful not to let ministry merely provide external information without delving into the inner springs and flow of the gifts of the Spirit.

22. Do the church and its servants today possess the heart of Christ to embrace sinners? If the Samaritan woman were to enter the church today, would we, in our pride, condemn her, or would we, like Jesus, stand humbly and say to her, "Give me a drink"?

23. When those being served recognise the abundance of wealth and glory bestowed upon them by God's presence in their lives, they overflow with joy and realise the depth of their strength. They understand that "there is none who is lame among them" (Acts 3:8). Instead, they are all strong, unshaken by the challenges of the times, and they inspire awe in the world with their holiness, courage, and purity, resembling an army with banners.

24. The priest carries his people on his shoulders and holds them in his heart.

25. The priest is a permanent agent of God, continuously offering prayer and sacrifice.

26. Ministry is a honour bestowed upon us, not because of our merit or favour from God.

27. Ministry is not a privilege of high positions; rather, it's a sharing in the burdens of the church.

28. Ministry is not about defending the church; it's about humbling oneself with the people of God and sharing in their experiences. Just as the Lord Jesus Himself, in flesh and blood, participated with His church and washed their feet.

29. There are four traits of the servant: love, fatherhood, humility and selflessness.

30. If ministry is driven by a desire to fill spare time, it won't fulfill the heart's emptiness; instead, it may lead to issues and stumbling blocks. However, when service is motivated by love for Christ, it becomes healthy and successful, and there's no concept of spare time.

Scan the QR code to go to our

website where you will find

- Book reviews

- Great deals

- Our full library of books